THE OFFICIAL
BIRMINGHAM
CITY
ANNUAL 2020

Written by Andy Greeves

Designed by Paul Galbraith and John Anderson

A Grange Publication

© 2019. Published by Grange Communications Ltd., Edinburgh, under licence from Birmingham City Football Club. Printed in the EU.

Photographs © Birmingham City Football Club and Roy Smiljanic.

ISBN: 978-1-913034-13-9

HELLO
BLUE NOSES!

WELCOME TO THE OFFICIAL BIRMINGHAM CITY ANNUAL 2020

In this annual, we'll profile the current playing squad and hear from star players such as Lee Camp, Maikel Kieftenbeld and Gary Gardner. We'll also take a look back on the 2018/19 season and discover what the team got up to at their pre-season training camp.

We'll dive into the history of Birmingham City and take a look at some of the kits the club have sported over the decades and discover how 'Keep Right On' became the club's anthem.

On top of that, there is a feature on some of the greatest goals scored by the club over the years while ahead of UEFA Euro 2020, there's a guide to various Blues that have represented their country at international level.

You can also find quizzes, games and fun facts along with some handy information on St. Andrew's Trillion Trophy Stadium.

Enjoy your new Annual and Keep Right On!

Andy Greeves

#Blues | #BCFC | #KRO

CONTENTS

A BRIEF HISTORY OF
BIRMINGHAM CITY FOOTBALL CLUB

BIRMINGHAM CITY WERE FORMED IN 1875 AS 'SMALL HEATH ALLIANCE' AND WERE RENAMED 'SMALL HEATH' IN 1888 AND 'BIRMINGHAM' IN 1905 BEFORE ASSUMING THE CLUB'S CURRENT NAME IN 1943.

Blues joined the Football Alliance for the 1889/90 season, which ran alongside the Football League. They joined the newly formed Football League Second Division in 1892 and were the division's inaugural champions, winning 17 of their 22 matches that season and losing just three games. They entered the First Division in 1894/95, achieving a respectable 12th place finish prior to relegation the following campaign.

After numerous promotions and relegations between the first and second tiers of the Football League, Blues enjoyed 18 consecutive seasons in the top flight between 1921 and 1939. The club reached their first-ever FA Cup Final during this period, going down to a 2-1 defeat to West Bromwich Albion at the original Wembley Stadium on 25 April 1931.

Birmingham City achieved their highest ever league finish in 1955/56, coming sixth in the old First Division. They got to the FA Cup Final that same season where they were beaten 3-1 by Manchester City at Wembley on 5 May 1956. Ten days later, they became the first-ever English club side to compete in a European competition, when they drew 0-0 away to Inter Milan in the Inter-Cities Fairs Cup. Continental football was very much to Blues' liking and the club reached the semi-

1896-97

ON 27 MAY 1963, BIRMINGHAM CITY CELEBRATED WINNING THE FIRST MAJOR TROPHY OF THEIR HISTORY

final of the competition in 1957/58 and got to the final in consecutive years in 1960 and 1961.

On 27 May 1963, Birmingham City celebrated winning the first major trophy of their history at the home ground of their arch-rivals, Aston Villa. Following a 3-1 victory over the Villains at St. Andrew's in the first leg of the League Cup Final on 23 May 1963 – which featured a brace from Ken Leek and a further strike from Jimmy Bloomfield – a goalless draw at Villa Park four days later secured Blues' triumph.

Birmingham City were relegated to the Second Division in 1965 but returned to the top flight in 1972, where they remained until 1979. The 1970s saw the emergence of a number of club legends, including Bob Latchford, who was the Second Division's top goal scorer in 1971/72 with 23 league strikes en route to the club's promotion. Trevor Francis was Blues' leading marksman for three consecutive campaigns between 1975 and 1978. When he was eventually sold to Nottingham Forest in 1979, he became the

1882-83

first English footballer to command a transfer fee of £1m.

The 1980s saw Blues yo-yo between the First and Second Divisions once again before suffering relegation to the third tier in 1989. The club won the Associate Members' Cup in 1991, beating Tranmere Rovers 3-2 in the final, before gaining promotion back to the second tier of English league football a year later.

IN 2001, BLUES GOT TO THE LEAGUE CUP FINAL AT CARDIFF'S MILLENNIUM STADIUM

BOB LATCHFORD

2ND DIVISION & FOOTBALL LEAGUE TROPHY

The 1994/95 season was a memorable one as Birmingham City won the Second Division (third tier) title and the Football League Trophy as Steve Claridge became the first Blues player to score 20 plus goals in a single campaign. The club went on an impressive run to the semi-finals of the League Cup the following season.

In 2001, Blues got to the League Cup Final at Cardiff's Millennium Stadium. After a 1-1 draw with Liverpool after extra-time, the Reds eventually triumphed 5-4 on penalties during a season in which they would also win the FA Cup and the UEFA Cup. Birmingham City returned to the Welsh capital just over 12 months later, enjoying their own penalty shootout success on that occasion. After a 1-1 draw with Norwich City in the Football League Championship Play-Off Final of 12 May 2002, Stern John, Paul Devlin, Stan Lazaridis and Darren Carter all scored from the spot as the club were promoted to the Premier League for the first time.

Blues achieved comfortable, mid-table finishes in the Premier League in their first three seasons in the division before suffering relegation in 2006. They bounced straight back to the top flight by virtue of a second-place finish in the Championship in 2007 and did so once again in 2009 having been relegated the previous year.

While Birmingham City dropped out of the Premier League once again in 2011, the year was still memorable as the club won the League Cup for the second time in their history. Strikes from Nikola Zigic and Obafemi Martins cancelled out Robin van Persie's opener in the 2-1 win over Arsenal at Wembley Stadium.

2ND DIVISION & FOOTBALL LEAGUE TROPHY

ASSOCIATE MEMBERS CUP

Currently in their ninth consecutive season in the EFL Championship, rarely has there been a dull moment in the history of Birmingham City Football Club...

FRANVILLALBA

BIRMINGHAM CITY
EFL CHAMPIONSHIP FIXTURES 2020

JANUARY
01 **WIGAN ATHLETIC** (H)
11 **LUTON TOWN** (A)
18 **CARDIFF CITY** (H)
25 **MIDDLESBROUGH** (A)

FEBRUARY
01 **NOTTINGHAM FOREST** (H)
08 **BRISTOL CITY** (A)
11 **BARNSLEY** (A)
15 **BRENTFORD** (H)
22 **SHEFFIELD WEDNESDAY** (H)
26 **MILLWALL** (A)
29 **QUEENS PARK RANGERS** (A)

MARCH
07 **READING** (H)
14 **WEST BROMWICH ALBION** (A)
18 **HULL CITY** (H)
21 **HUDDERSFIELD TOWN** (H)

APRIL
04 **FULHAM** (A)
10 **SWANSEA CITY** (H)
13 **STOKE CITY** (A)
18 **CHARLTON ATHLETIC** (H)
25 **PRESTON NORTH END** (A)

MAY
02 **DERBY COUNTY** (H)

FIXTURE DATES ARE SUBJECT TO CHANGE
VISIT **WWW.BCFC.COM**
FOR AN UP-TO-DATE FIXTURE LIST

REVIEW 2018/19
EFL CHAMPIONSHIP

THE 2018/19 SEASON MARKED BIRMINGHAM CITY'S EIGHTH
CONSECUTIVE SEASON IN THE EFL CHAMPIONSHIP.

LEEDS

STOKE CITY

Blues side drew 2-2 with Norwich City at St. Andrew's Trillion Trophy Stadium on the opening day of the campaign thanks to strikes from Jacques Maghoma and Viv Solomon-Otabor.

Blues drew six of their eight opening fixtures of the season before picking up their first victory at Leeds United in September. Che Adams' brace in the 2-1 win at Elland Road came during a campaign in which the striker netted 22 times in the league. Lukas Jutkiewicz got the first hat-trick of the season in a 3-1 win for Monk's side at home to Rotherham United a month later.

October was an excellent month for Blues, who won all four of their Championship fixtures. After seeing off the Millers, victories were achieved against Stoke City (1-0), Reading (2-1) and Sheffield Wednesday (3-1).

Adams got a hat-trick in a 3-3 draw at home to Hull City in December, before the first Second City Derby of the season ended in a 4-2 away defeat at Aston Villa. Blues quickly bounced back from that disappointment with a run of form that saw them head up the table towards the Championship's play-off places. Four wins, two draws and just one defeat from 28 November 2018 through to the end of the year moved Monk's side into seventh position in the league.

ROTHERHAM

HULL CITY

QPR

LEEDS

BLUES SHOWED THEIR RESOLVE IN THE FINAL MONTHS OF THE CAMPAIGN

At the start of 2019, Adams scored in six consecutive league matches. He got eight goals in total during this run, including a hat-trick in a dramatic 4-3 win at Queens Park Rangers in February. A 2-1 victory at Bristol City towards the end of the month kept Blues in contention for a play-off place but five back-to-back defeats – including a 1-0 loss to Aston Villa - in March all but ended those hopes.

Blues showed their resolve in the final months of the campaign, going seven matches unbeaten. That excellent run of form began in early April with a 1-0 win over a Leeds United side that made it into the play-offs at the end of the season. Credible draws with current Premier League outfit Sheffield United and play-off finalists Derby County followed that month while Swedish international Kerim Mrabti scored his first goal in a 3-1 triumph at Rotherham United.

The last home match of the season saw Blues draw 1-1 with Wigan Athletic while the campaign ended with a goalless match with Reading at the Madejski Stadium.

BRISTOL CITY

BRISTOL CITY

WIGAN

CUP MATCH REVIEW 2018-19

CARABAO CUP

Garry Monk handed Blues debuts to **Lee Camp**, **Dan Scarr** and **Gary Gardner** and first starts for **Connor Mahoney, Beryly Lubala** and **Omar Bogle** in his side's Carabao Cup first round tie at Reading. The home side ran out comfortable 2-0 winners on the night, thanks to goals from **Yakou Meite** and **John Swift**.

FA CUP

Birmingham City were handed a tricky FA Cup third round tie, as they were drawn away to Premier League side West Ham United. After **Marko Arnautovic**'s early goal for the Hammers, Monk's team missed several chances to level, with **Lukas Jutkiewicz** coming close on a number of occasions. Blues were punished with **Andy Carroll**'s injury-time header sealing a 2-0 win for the home side in front of a crowd of 54,840.

FA YOUTH CUP

Having reached the semi-final of the FA Youth Cup the previous season, much was expected of Blues' Under-18 side as they entered the 2018/19 competition. Alas, they went down to a 1-0 away defeat at Watford in the third round, with **Sonny Blu Lo-Everton** scoring the Hornets' winner in the match played at Wingate & Finchley's Maurice Rebak Stadium.

CHAMPIONSHIP TABLE 2018-19

Pos	Team	Pld	W	D	L	GF	GA	GD	Pts
1	NORWICH CITY	46	27	13	6	93	57	+36	94
2	SHEFFIELD UNITED	46	26	11	9	78	41	+37	89
3	LEEDS UNITED	46	25	8	13	73	50	+23	83
4	WEST BROMWICH ALBION	46	23	11	12	87	62	+25	80
5	ASTON VILLA	46	20	16	10	82	61	+21	76
6	DERBY COUNTY	46	20	14	12	69	54	+15	74
7	MIDDLESBROUGH	46	20	13	13	49	41	+8	73
8	BRISTOL CITY	46	19	13	14	59	53	+6	70
9	NOTTINGHAM FOREST	46	17	15	14	61	54	+7	66
10	SWANSEA CITY	46	18	11	17	65	62	+3	65
11	BRENTFORD	46	17	13	16	73	59	+14	64
12	SHEFFIELD WEDNESDAY	46	16	16	14	60	62	−2	64
13	HULL CITY	46	17	11	18	66	68	−2	62
14	PRESTON NORTH END	46	16	13	17	67	67	0	61
15	BLACKBURN ROVERS	46	16	12	18	64	69	−5	60
16	STOKE CITY	46	11	22	13	45	52	−7	55
17	BIRMINGHAM CITY	46	14	19	13	64	58	+6	52
18	WIGAN ATHLETIC	46	13	13	20	51	64	−13	52
19	QUEENS PARK RANGERS	46	14	9	23	53	71	−18	51
20	READING	46	10	17	19	49	66	−17	47
21	MILLWALL	46	10	14	22	48	64	−16	44
22	ROTHERHAM UNITED	46	8	16	22	52	83	−31	40
23	BOLTON WANDERERS	46	8	8	30	29	78	−49	32
24	IPSWICH TOWN	46	5	16	25	36	77	−41	31

INTERVIEW
GARY GARDNER

HAVING SPENT A SUCCESSFUL SEASON ON LOAN WITH BIRMINGHAM CITY IN 2018/19, GARY GARDNER SEALED A PERMANENT MOVE TO ST. ANDREW'S TRILLION TROPHY STADIUM IN THE SUMMER OF 2019.

Having grown up supporting **Birmingham City,** Gary Gardner completed a dream transfer in the summer of 2019 as he signed permanently for the club from rivals Aston Villa. The midfielder spent the 2018/19 season on loan at St. Andrew's Trillion Trophy Stadium, where he was a regular in the starting line-up, featuring in 42 Blues matches and scoring two goals.

"What really stood out was a togetherness and a willingness to work hard and to perform in every game and on the training pitch. We can obviously improve but I thought we had a good season." commented Gardner when asked about his highlights of the 2018/19 campaign.

"Our ambitions as a team going forward would be to make the Play-Offs or promotion... to go up any way we can. Personally, my aim is to try and score a few more goals and help the team in that way. I'm just looking to carry

on with what I did last season (2018/19) and improve on things."

Gary is the younger brother of fellow Birmingham City midfielder Craig Gardner, who is currently in his second spell at St. Andrew's. Craig originally represented the club in the Premier League for two seasons between 2009 and 2011. After spells with Sunderland and West Bromwich Albion, he returned to the club, initially on loan, in 2017.

"THE EXPERIENCE OF PLAYING AGAINST DIFFERENT COUNTRIES - WITH AND AGAINST TOP PLAYERS - YOU LEARN A LOT FROM THAT."

"Growing up, I'd play football over the park with him (Craig) and my other brothers," smiles Gary. "It's surreal going from playing down the park to being on the professional stage with the club we both supported as kids.

"He (Craig) didn't really have to say anything during my loan spell (about joining Birmingham City permanently), he knew my thoughts. It's been brilliant having him here. It helped me settle in really well. To have my brother, who has so much experience in the game and around the Club, has been a real help if I ever need advice. He's always there to help me and it's had a massive impact on me."

Gary has a wealth of experience himself, having played nearly 200 professional club matches, at the time of writing. He made 16 Premier League appearances during his time in the Aston Villa first-team between 2011

and 2018 and he has played for six different clubs at EFL Championship level, including Blues. As a youngster, he also featured for England at Under-17, Under-19 and Under-20 level and scored twice in five appearances for the Three Lions' Under-21 side between 2011 and 2012.

"THE WHOLE THING OF PLAYING FOR YOUR COUNTRY IS A BIG HONOUR."

"The experience of playing against different countries - with and against top players - you learn a lot from that," reflects Gary on his international career. "The whole thing of playing for your country is a big honour."

Those fortunate to have watched Gary play will be fully aware of his qualities as a midfielder. He is a tough tackler who is strong in the air, has a good range of passing and the ability to pop up in the penalty area to score important goals. Like many players, Gary has a matchday ritual – putting his left sock and boot on before the right one – while away from football, he loves nothing more than spending time with his family and playing the occasional round of golf!

PLAYER FACTS

Full Name: **Gary Gardner**
Date of Birth: **29 June 1992**
Place of Birth: **Solihull**
Position: **Midfielder**
Height (m): **1.85m**
Previous Club(s): **Aston Villa, Coventry City (loan), Sheffield Wednesday (loan), Brighton & Hove Albion (loan), Nottingham Forest (loan), Barnsley (loan)**

INTERVIEW
LEE CAMP

GOALKEEPER LEE CAMP BECAME A REAL FANS' FAVOURITE DURING HIS DEBUT SEASON WITH BIRMINGHAM CITY IN 2018/19 WITH HIS CONSISTENT PERFORMANCES AND SPECTACULAR SAVES.

Birmingham City are the eleventh club of Lee Camp's career, with the goalkeeper having originally started out on loan with then-Conference side Burton Albion before making his Football League debut for Derby County at Walsall back in April 2003. Since then, he has twice been part of teams that have gained promotion, featuring in the Queens Park Rangers side that finished runners-up in the old Second Division in 2003/04 and AFC Bournemouth's EFL Championship-winning team of 2014/15.

"I've managed to represent both England Under-21s and Northern Ireland (at senior international level)," said Camp, reflecting on his career highlights to date. "They were two different but great experiences. I played in different countries and in the Euro 2012 qualifiers. They were good experiences that I look back on fondly. I've also played in the Premier League (for Norwich City in 2012/13)."

Lee won a total of five caps for England Under-21s between 2004 and 2007 before switching his international allegiance and making nine appearances for Northern Ireland between 2011 and 2012. He was voted his club's Player of the Year during spells at Nottingham Forest and Rotherham United and he was selected in the PFA's Championship Team of the Year in 2009/10 as he featured in all but one of Forest's league matches as they came third in the division.

He made a real impression at Birmingham City in his first season at St. Andrew's in 2018/19, appearing in all but two of the club's EFL Championship matches during the campaign and playing in 46 matches overall. His career at St. Andrew's Trillion Trophy Stadium got off to a great start and he kept a clean sheet on his competitive Blues debut in a goalless draw with Swansea City in August 2018.

"IN THE FIRST GAME YOU OBVIOUSLY WANT TO MAKE A VERY GOOD IMPRESSION AND THERE'S NO BETTER WAY FOR A GOALKEEPER TO DO THAT (THAN BY KEEPING A CLEAN SHEET),"

"In the first game you obviously want to make a very good impression and there's no better way for a goalkeeper to do that (than by keeping a clean sheet)," commented Camp on his shutout against the Welsh club. "We played well as a team that night."

"Overall, the team made good progress last season. It was obviously a difficult year for one reason or another but we did well to recover from the points deduction and we were pushing for the top six at one stage."

Lee kept clean sheets in three of his opening six Championship matches for Blues in 2018/19 – with 12 shutouts in total during the campaign. He wrote his name into Birmingham

City folklore with an excellent display at Queens Park Rangers in February 2019, where he made a string of fine saves and kept out a stoppage-time penalty from Nahki Wells to seal a 4-3 win. It was around that time that supporters started chanting 'Lee Camp, in the middle of our goal' to the tune of Our House by Madness.

"I WANT TO PLAY AS HIGH AS I CAN UP THE LEAGUES FOR AS LONG AS POSSIBLE, AND AS LONG AS I CAN DO A JOB."

"That was nice," smiled Camp, discussing Blues supporters' musical tribute to him. "The fans were great to us all season with their backing… they can play a big part for us. It is appreciated by the players."

Lee will celebrate his 36th birthday in August 2020 but has no plans to retire just yet. "I want to keep going as long as I can," confirmed the former Northern Ireland stopper. "I want to play as high as I can up the leagues for as long as possible, and as long as I can do a job. That's the most important thing. I don't want to just hang around. I think I'll know within myself (when it's the right time to retire)."

For any aspirational young goalkeepers reading this Annual meanwhile, Lee offers the following advice: "Seek out good coaching, learn good technique and positioning and get the fundamentals down to a tee."

PLAYER FACTS

Full Name: **Lee Michael John Camp**
Date of Birth: **22 August 1984**
Place of Birth: **Derby**
Position: **Goalkeeper**
Height(m): **1.83m**
Previous Club(s): **Derby County, Burton Albion (loan), Queens Park Rangers (loan), Nottingham Forest, Norwich City, West Bromwich Albion, AFC Bournemouth, Rotherham United, Cardiff City, Sunderland (loan)**

INTERVIEW
MAIKEL KIEFTENBELD

DUTCHMAN MAIKEL KIEFTENBELD TALKS TO OFFICIAL BIRMINGHAM CITY ANNUAL 2020 EDITOR ANDY GREEVES ABOUT THE ENJOYMENT HE HAS GAINED FROM HIS TIME WITH BLUES SO FAR...

Since his arrival at St. Andrew's Trillion Trophy Stadium, Maikel Kieftenbeld has become part of the furniture at Birmingham City, having featured in 163 matches in his first four seasons at the club.

The Dutch midfielder rose through the ranks at Eredivisie side FC Twente before making his senior debut at Go Ahead Eagles, for whom he scored three goals in 72 appearances between 2008 and 2010. He then went to play in 171 FC Groningen matches – netting four times in five seasons - before fulfilling a career ambition by signing for Blues in July 2015.

"I always wanted to go to England," comments the midfielder. "I have enjoyed my time with Blues. We play in a good league, with good competition and the players have a great mentality. You always see the passion of the fans… that has been brilliant. Yes, we have had some tough seasons but overall I have a good experience."

Prior to sustaining a knee injury in Blues' 1-0 home victory over Leeds United in April 2019, which saw him ruled out for a significant period of time, 'Kieft' was one of the first names on the manager's team sheet. The Dutchman plays two important roles in Birmingham City's midfield – protecting the backline and supporting the team's attacking play.

"YOU ALWAYS SEE THE PASSION OF THE FANS... THAT HAS BEEN BRILLIANT."

"The Manager gave me a job to do in the team I really liked," reflects Maikel on his performances for Blues in 2018/19, that saw him make 38 appearances in all competitions, who scored once in a 3-0 win over Preston North End in December 2018. "In the past some managers played me in different roles. I think I played more good games than bad games. It was the same for the team. We did well, expectations of us was that we might be going down but we were fighting a long time for the Play-Offs. Because of my injury at the end of the season, it was a bad way to end the campaign on a personal level."

As well as relishing his responsibilities on the pitch, Maikel has adapted well to life away from the football field during his time at Birmingham City.

"Birmingham is really up and coming as a city," says Kieft, who featured in a series of videos for BluesTV in 2018 that saw him explore the sights of England's second city.

"It's a perfect city for me because family can come over easily. I live in the centre and there are nice restaurants, nice areas."

Maikel had the honour of representing his country, the Netherlands, at Under-21 level. He won five caps for the 'Jong Oranje' between 2010 and 2011 and was also included in their squad for the 2012 Toulon Tournament alongside players including Ajax's Joel Veltman and Davy Propper, who currently plies his trade for Premier League Brighton & Hove Albion.

"BIRMINGHAM IS REALLY UP AND COMING AS A CITY,"

"I was really proud," reflects Maikel on his appearances for the Netherlands' Under-21s. "But it was weird because they had a lot of good midfielders. Then I went to Groningen and played my first season there at right-back. So, what happened was that the Under-21s didn't have a right-back and I got called up for that position. To listen to the national anthem when you are lining up, it is a special feeling and I played alongside some special players."

Speaking of special players, Blues supporters view Maikel Kieftenbeld as just that. After damaging the anterior cruciate ligament in his right knee in the aforementioned match against Leeds United, Bluenoses will be hoping 2020 marks Kieft's long-awaited return to full fitness.

PLAYER FACTS

Full Name: **Maikel Kieftenbeld**
Date of Birth: **26 June 1990**
Place of Birth: **Lemelerveld, Netherlands**
Position: **Midfielder**
Height(m): **1.79m**
Previous Club(s): **Go Ahead Eagles, FC Groningen**

MEMORABLE
GOALS

FROM VOLLEYS AND HEADERS TO LONG-RANGE PILE-DRIVERS AND SOLO EFFORTS, EDITOR ANDY GREEVES TAKES A LOOK AT SOME OF THE MOST IMPRESSIVE AND IMPORTANT GOALS IN BIRMINGHAM CITY'S HISTORY.

1 JOHN CONNOLLY v ASTON VILLA (away)
18 September 1976

A fluent passing move involving Trevor Francis and Howard Kendall ended in a remarkable, long-range goal from John Connolly in Blues' 2-1 victory against rivals Aston Villa in September 1976. After collecting the ball just inside the Villa half, Connolly rode three challenges before firing a shot beyond the despairing dive of Villains' keeper John Burridge from some 25 yards.

TREVOR FRANCIS v QUEENS PARK RANGERS (home)
30 October 1976

2

The BBC *Match of the Day* cameras were at St. Andrew's to capture one of Trevor Francis' best goals for Birmingham City in a 2-1 win against Queens Park Rangers in October 1976. Collecting a throw-in at the edge of the Hoops penalty area, Francis turned marker Frank McLintock inside-out and bypassed Mick Leach before curling a left-footed shot past goalkeeper Phil Parkes from a tight angle. "That was intrinsic skill," remarked commentator John Motson on the forward's effort.

3 LOUIE DONOWA v WEST BROMWICH ALBION (away)
27 April 1994

During a struggling season that saw Birmingham City relegated to the old Second Division, Barry Fry's team provided Bluenoses with a rare moment of joy with a 4-2 win away at rivals West Bromwich Albion. Steve Claridge got two goals in the victory while Andy Saville was also on target. The most memorable strike of all that night, though, came from midfielder Louie Donowa. With the score at 1-1 at the time, Claridge raced onto a long ball from Scott Hiley. Albion number one Stuart Naylor came out of his penalty area to head clear but Donowa collected the loose ball and lobbed the goalkeeper from some 35 yards.

STAN LAZARIDIS v EVERTON (home)
11 February 2004

4

Birmingham City were leading 1-0 in their Premier League match when Australian international Stan Lazaridis set off on a run with the ball from inside his own half. With no immediate challenge coming in, he continued to move at pace into the Toffees' penalty area before beating Nigel Martyn with a shot from a tight angle with six minutes of the first half remaining. After one of the finest individual goals ever seen at St. Andrew's, Mikael Forssell netted four minutes after the break to wrap up a 3-0 victory.

5 SEBASTIAN LARSSON v TOTTENHAM HOTSPUR (away)
2 December 2007

With Blues drawing 2-2 at Tottenham Hotspur in stoppage time at the end of the 90 minutes, Sebastian Larsson chose the ideal moment to hit a memorable winner. After making a fine tackle on Spurs' Bulgarian striker Dimitar Berbatov, the Swede ran onto the loose ball and hit it first-time from 30 yards. The shot rose and swerved into the top corner, giving England international goalkeeper Paul Robinson no chance of stopping it.

MEMORABLE GOALS

6 CAMERON JEROME v LIVERPOOL (away)
9 November 2009

Cameron Jerome's strike in Birmingham City's 2-2 draw at Anfield was voted BBC Match of the Day's 'Goal of the Month' for November 2009. In the third minute of stoppage time at the end of the first-half, the Huddersfield-born forward hit a long-range shot over the head of Spanish international goalkeeper Pepe Reina. Commentator Jon Champion declared; "there won't be many (goals) better that in the Premier League all season long".

OBAFEMI MARTINS v ARSENAL (Wembley) 7
27 February 2011

Obafemi Martins capitalised on a defensive mix-up between Arsenal goalkeeper Wojciech Szczesny and defender Laurent Koscielny to score the winning goal for Blues in the final minute of 2011 League Cup Final. While the finish was a simple one, the goal is included in this list for its sheer importance in Birmingham City's history.

8 EMYR HUWS v MIDDLESBROUGH (away)
8 April 2014

Emyr Huws joined Birmingham City on loan from Manchester City for the second half of the 2013/14 season. The Welsh midfielder scored two memorable goals in his 17 league appearances for the club, including a thunderous 35-yard drive at Middlesbrough that was subsequently voted the club's 'Goal of the Season'.

PAUL CADDIS v BOLTON WANDERERS (away)
3 May 2014

Requiring at least a draw to escape relegation to League One on the final day of the 2013/14 season, things didn't look good for Lee Clarke's Birmingham City as they trailed 2-0 at Bolton Wanderers with only 12 minutes of the match remaining. Nikola Zigic gave Blues hope with a late header before Paul Caddis popped up with a crucial equaliser in the third minute of stoppage time.

10 JEREMIE BOGA v SHEFFIELD UNITED (away)
25 November 2017

Jeremie Boga scored an incredible opener in Blues' 1-1 draw at Sheffield United in November 2017. After a corner was headed clear by a Blades defender, Boga controlled the ball with his chest before rifling a shot into the back of the net from some 25 yards out.

SHARP
SHOOTER!

INTRODUCING BLUES' NUMBER TEN, LUKAS JUTKIEWICZ.

Lukas Isaac Paul Jutkiewicz was **born in Southampton** on 28 March 1989 and joined Southampton Football Club's Academy aged ten having impressed Saints scouts with his performances in the Tyro League for the likes of Eastleigh Earls and Winsor.

After three years with the Hampshire club, Jutkiewicz joined Swindon Town, and made his professional debut in a 2-1 defeat at Swansea City on 11 April 2006. He was just 17 years of age at the time. He featured in five matches for the Robins towards the end of the 2005/06 season and did enough in those games to be presented with the club's Young Player of the Year Award at the end of the campaign.

Jutkiewicz netted five times in 33 League Two appearances for Swindon in 2006/07, as the Wiltshire side gained promotion by virtue of a third-place finish in the division. Premier League club Everton agreed to sign the striker at the end of that campaign. He made his debut for the Toffees as a substitute against Sunderland in December 2008 in what proved to be his one and only competitive, first-team appearance for the club.

During his time at Goodison Park, Jutkiewicz was sent out on loan to Plymouth Argyle, Huddersfield Town and Motherwell. He did particularly well in Scotland, scoring 12 goals in 33 Scottish Premier League matches for the Well during the 2010/11 season. The following campaign saw the forward signed for Coventry City on a permanent deal, for whom he netted 18 times in 69 appearances between 2010 and 2012.

THE STRIKER BECAME A BLUE IN AUGUST 2016, INITIALLY SIGNING FOR BIRMINGHAM CITY ON LOAN FROM BURNLEY

Jutkiewicz joined Middlesbrough in January 2012, scoring the first of his 15 goals for Boro in an FA Cup fourth round replay against Sunderland the following month. He was loaned to Bolton Wanderers for part of the 2013/14 season, where he bagged seven goals in 20 Championship matches. He became a Premier League player for the first time in 2014, joining newly-promoted Burnley after 71 appearances in two-and-a-half seasons with Boro.

Jutkiewicz made a total of 35 appearances for Burnley between 2014 and 2016, but failed to score during his time at Turf Moor. The striker became a Blue in August 2016, initially signing for Birmingham City on loan from Burnley. He made his debut for the club as a second-half substitute in a 1-0 away win at Fulham on 10 September 2016. His first goal arrived a week later as he headed the winner in Blues' 2-1 victory over Sheffield Wednesday. His transfer to St. Andrew's was made permanent a few months later.

Jutkiewicz's 12 goals in 40 appearances for Birmingham City in his debut season in 2016/17 made him the club's top goal scorer. He also made a number of a vital assists that season, including the pass that set-up Che Adams to score the only goal of the game, in a 1-0 away win at Bristol City on 7 May 2017 that maintained Blues' place in the EFL Championship.

JUTKIEWICZ'S 12 GOALS IN 40 APPEARANCES FOR BIRMINGHAM CITY IN HIS DEBUT SEASON MADE HIM THE CLUB'S TOP GOAL SCORER.

The Southampton-born forward followed that up with six goals in 38 appearances for Birmingham City in all competitions in 2017/18 prior to his most productive season to date in 2018/19. His 14 strikes in 47 matches last campaign saw him named as both the Who Scored and Sky Sports Power Rankings' EFL Championship Player of the Season. He was one of only a handful of players to get into double figures for both goals and assists during the campaign.

Jutkiewicz scored his first professional hat-trick in Blues' 3-1 home victory over Rotherham United on 6 October 2018, having bagged a brace against Ipswich Town in his previous St Andrew's appearance. He put pen-to-paper on a new contract in July 2019, committing his future to Blues until the summer of 2022. As of the end of the 2018/19 season, the striker had managed 32 goals in 125 Birmingham City matches.

ON THE INTERNATIONAL STAGE

EDITOR ANDY GREEVES TAKES A LOOK AT A SELECTION OF BIRMINGHAM CITY PLAYERS PAST AND PRESENT WHO HAVE REPRESENTED THEIR COUNTRY AT FULL INTERNATIONAL LEVEL.

When **Caesar Jenkyns made his debut for Wales against Ireland on 27 February 1892,** he became the first Birmingham City (then Small Heath) player to win a senior international cap. The Builth Wells-born defender made eight appearances for the Dragons between 1892 and 1898.

Jenkyns is one of a number of Welsh players to represent their country whilst at Birmingham City – **Malcolm Page, Terry Hennessey, Colin Green, Billy Hughes, Ken Leek, David Cotterill, Noel Kinsey, Ernie Curtis, Wilson Jones, Don Dearson** and **Tony Rees** are amongst a list of other former Blues to have turned out for the Dragons.

At the time of writing, 18 Blues have represented England at full international level. The first of these was goalkeeper **Chris Charsley**, who made his one and only appearance for the Three Lions in a 6-1 win over Ireland on 25 February 1893.

Ex-Birmingham City player **Watty Corbett** was part of the Great Britain side that won gold at the 1908 Olympic Games. He also won three England caps that year with appearances against Austria, Hungary and Bohemia all coming within the space of seven days.

Left-half **Percy Barton** collected all seven of his England caps as a Birmingham City player while all 12 of **Joe Bradford**'s appearances and his seven goals for the Three Lions came as a Blue Nose. Goalkeeper **Dan Tremlling**'s one and only international appearance

CAESAR JENKYNS

AT THE TIME OF WRITING, 18 BLUES HAVE REPRESENTED ENGLAND AT FULL INTERNATIONAL LEVEL.

came against Wales in 1927 while **Lewis Stoker** featured in three England matches between 1932 and 1943 and **Tommy Grosvenor** scored two goals in three internationals in 1933.

Blues' most capped England international is goalkeeper **Harry Hibbs**, who started 25 matches for his country between 1929 and 1936. Fellow stopper **Gil Merrick** holds the distinction of being the first Birmingham City player to feature at the World Cup. He started in the Three Lions' matches against Belgium, hosts Switzerland

HARRY HIBBS

GIL MERRICK

TREVOR FRANCIS

MATT UPSON

MAIK TAYLOR

SEB LARSSON

and Uruguay at the 1954 tournament. Merrick was a one-club man, who played 12 times for England between 1951 and 1954.

Jeff Hall, Gordon Astall and **Trevor Smith** featured for both Birmingham City and England during the 1950s while **Mike Hellawell** collected two caps in 1962. **Trevor Francis** enjoyed a distinguished career with England scoring 12 goals in 52 matches between 1977 and 1986. 12 of those appearances - including his debut against the Netherlands - and two goals came as a Blue Nose.

Matthew Upson became the first Blues player to represent England in nearly quarter of a century when he made his international debut as a substitute for Rio Ferdinand in a 2-1 friendly victory in South Africa in 2003. Seven of his 21 international appearances came whilst representing Birmingham City. During their time with Blues, **Emile Heskey, Ben Foster** and **Jack Butland** also featured for the Three Lions.

Maik Taylor is Birmingham City's most capped player of all-time. The goalkeeper won 58 of his 88 caps for Northern Ireland during his time at St. Andrew's between 2004 and 2011. Fellow Northern Irishman **Damien Johnson** featured in 42 internationals as a Blue between 2002 and 2010 while **Jon McCarthy** and **Ray Ferris** also turned out for the Green and White Army. Amongst the list of Birmingham City's former Scottish internationals are **Johnny Crosbie, Kenny Burns, Des Bremner, Paul Caddid, Chris Burke, Paul Devlin, Archie Gemmill** and **Neil Dougall**. The Republic of Ireland meanwhile has been represented by Blues favourites such as **Kenny Cunningham, Keith Fahey, Stephen Gleeson** and **Dave Langan**.

Birmingham City have been served by two Swedish internationals during their history. **Seb Larsson** – who has now won over 100 caps for his country – made 31 appearances for his country during his time at St. Andrew's between 2006 and 2011. Current Blue Nose **Kerim Mrabti** had been capped three times by the Scandinavian nation, as of the end of the 2018/19 season.

BLUES' MOST CAPPED ENGLAND INTERNATIONAL IS GOALKEEPER HARRY HIBBS, WHO STARTED 25 MATCHES FOR HIS COUNTRY BETWEEN 1929 AND 1936.

Mikael Forssell and **Nikola Zigic** turned out for Finland and Serbia respectively during their stay with Birmingham City, while **Stan Lazaridis** was capped 33 times by Australia whilst at the club between 1999 and 2006.

Martin O'Connor represented the Cayman Islands, **Jonathan Spector** was a full United States international and Peter Ndlovu collected 12 caps for Zimbabwe whilst playing for Blues. **Clayton Donaldson** and **Michael Johnson** collected 33 and 12 caps respectively for Jamaica while under contract at St. Andrew's.

Current midfielder **Jacques Maghoma** has played international football for the Democratic Republic of Congo since 2010 with 19 caps to his name, as of the end of the 2018/19 season.

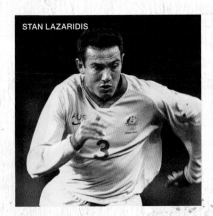
STAN LAZARIDIS

PETER NDLOVU

JACQUES MAGHOMA

KEEP RIGHT ON
CLUB ANTHEM

EDITOR ANDY GREEVES DISCOVERS THE ORIGINS OF BIRMINGHAM CITY'S FAMOUS ANTHEM 'KEEP RIGHT ON'.

'Keep Right On', or 'Keep Right On to the End of the Road' to give it its full title, was written by Sir Henry 'Harry' Lauder after the death his son, Captain John C. Lauder, who was killed in action during World War I.

Born in Edinburgh in 1870, Harry was the eldest of eight children. He was just 12 years old when he and his siblings were orphaned, leaving him no option but to work in the local flax mill to make ends meet. He worked as a coal miner in his early teens, when he began to sing to bolster his spirits when he was down the mine. Encouraged by his fellow miners, the Scot began to enter local singing contests.

Harry enjoyed a rapid rise as a singer/songwriter and comedian, eventually becoming the highest paid entertainer of his day and the first British artist to sell a million records. By 1928, he had sold a million more. Former British Prime Minister Sir Winston Churchill once described Lauder as "Scotland's greatest ever ambassador".

Harry used to perform 'Keep Right On' at the end of each of his wartime shows and eventually recorded and released it with American artist William Dillion in 1924. He passed away on 26 February 1950 at the age of 79, leaving behind a legacy of fine Scottish music and numerous films, including one titled 'The End of the Road' (1936).

FORMER BRITISH PRIME MINISTER SIR WINSTON CHURCHILL ONCE DESCRIBED LAUDER AS "SCOTLAND'S GREATEST EVER AMBASSADOR"

There are numerous stories about how 'Keep Right On' became Birmingham City's anthem, but it is generally agreed that Scottish winger Alex Govan was the man who introduced it to the club during Blues' run to the FA Cup Final in 1955/56. As Blues travelled to various away matches during that season, it became a tradition for the players to sing on the team bus – a ritual engineered by then-manager Arthur Turner.

Govan once offered his take on how 'Keep Right On' became adopted by Birmingham City players and supporters during that FA Cup journey in 1956…

"After beating Albion in the fifth round, we were drawn against the mighty Arsenal in the quarter final, not an easy prospect in those days either," explained Govan, who

passed away in June 2016 aged 86.

"We left our hotel at Hendon for the short journey to (Arsenal's then-home ground) Highbury and as usual, after just a few yards down the road we were lifting the roof off the coach!

"I remember singing a couple of Scottish favourites as my 'party piece', one of which was 'Keep Right On to the End of the Road'. The skipper, Len Boyd, was belting out 'Any Old Iron' for the umpteenth time when the gaffer bellowed up the coach, 'Let's have one from Scotland, Alex'. I duly obliged with 'Keep Right On to the End of the Road' once again. This time some of the other lads joined in the chorus and one by one they quickly caught onto the words, we sang it again and again until the entire coach was rocking as we pulled up outside Highbury!

"THE ENTIRE COACH WAS ROCKING AS WE PULLED UP OUTSIDE HIGHBURY!"

"I remember the coach was one of the older types which had wind down windows alongside the seats. It was a warm day so all the lads had their windows down and with the strains of 'Keep Right On' going at full belt, the Blues fans who always congregated outside the ground to welcome us to away games could hear us coming several streets away! They had picked up on the words too and were all singing it as we filed off the coach."

By the time Birmingham City took to the field at Wembley Stadium for the FA Cup Final against Manchester City on 5 May 1956, 'Keep Right On' had become well established as Blues anthem. Indeed, it was included in the pre-match community singing as a tribute to Blues, while 'She's a Lassie from Lancashire' was sung in respect of the Citizens. Alas, the regular renditions of Sir Harry Lauder's famous lyrics throughout the match failed to prevent Blues going down to a 3-1 defeat that afternoon.

'Keep Right On' has been sung by Birmingham City supporters for over 60 years now. In that time, the opening verse of 'Keep Right On' has been slightly modified by Blues fans from Lauder's original words while a couple of lines in the chorus have changed over time too.

Just as any football fan will think of Manchester City when they hear 'Blue Moon' or West Ham United when they listen to 'I'm Forever Blowing Bubbles', 'Keep Right On' will forever be synonymous with Birmingham City Football Club.

'KEEP RIGHT ON' LYRICS: *as sung by Blues fans today*

Verse One:
As you go through life it's a long, long road
There'll be joys and sorrows too
As we journey on we will sing this song
For the boys in Royal Blue.
We're often partisan - la la la
We will journey on - la la la

Chorus:
Keep right on to the end of the road
Keep right on to the end
Though the way be long let your heart beat strong
Keep right on to the end
Though you're tired and weary
Still journey on 'til you come to your happy abode
With all our love we'll be dreaming of
We'll be there at the end of the road.
Birmingham, Birmingham.

PLAYER

LEE
CAMP

Lee made 46 appearances for Blues in his debut season at St. Andrew's in 2018/19 and featured in all but two of the club's EFL Championship matches during the campaign. The former England Under-21 goalkeeper switched his international allegiance at senior level in 2011 and went on to win nine caps for Northern Ireland.

WES
HARDING

Wes had featured in 41 Blues matches by the end of the 2018/19 season. The Leicester-born defender was the winner of the club's Young Player of the Season for 2017/18, the campaign in which he made his senior debut against Crawley Town in the Football League Cup.

PROFILES

KRISTIAN
PEDERSEN

Signed from German side Union Berlin in June 2018, Kristian made 39 EFL Championship appearances for Blues in his debut season with the club. The former Denmark Under-21 defender scored his first Birmingham City goal in a 4-2 defeat at Aston Villa in November 2018.

MARC
ROBERTS

Marc suffered a hamstring injury in Blues' 2-2 draw at Blackburn Rovers in December 2018 that saw him ruled out until after the March 2019 international break. The defender was therefore restricted to just nine Blues appearances in 2018/19 having featured in 35 games the previous campaign.

MAXIME
COLIN

Having signed from Brentford in the summer of 2017, Maxime established himself as a regular starter in his first two seasons with Birmingham City. The former France Under-20 right-back scored two goals in 36 matches for the club in 2017/18 and followed that up with 44 appearances for Blues in 2018/19.

MAIKEL
KIEFTENBELD

Maikel was an almost ever-present in Blues' starting line-up in his first four seasons at the club, featuring in no fewer than 163 matches from the beginning of 2015/16 through until the end of the 2018/19 campaign. The former Dutch Under-21 midfielder has five years of top flight experience, having turned out for Eredivisie club Groningen between 2010 and 2015.

DAN
CROWLEY

Former Arsenal trainee Dan signed for Blues in the summer of 2019 from Dutch club Willem II. The Coventry-born midfielder was loaned to Barnsley, Oxford United and Go Ahead Eagles during his time at the Emirates Stadium while he also represented SC Cambuur on loan whilst at Willem II. He made his Birmingham City debut in a 1-0 win at Brentford on the opening day of the 2019/20 EFL Championship season.

CRAIG
GARDNER

Craig is one of Birmingham City's longest serving players, having originally represented the club in the Premier League for two seasons between 2009 and 2011. After spells with Sunderland and West Bromwich Albion, he returned to St. Andrew's – initially on loan – in 2017. As of the end of the 2018/19 season, he had netted 17 times in 124 Blues matches during his career.

LUKAS
JUTKIEWICZ

Lukas was an important source of goals for Blues during the 2018/19 season, with 14 strikes in 47 appearances in all competitions. The forward scored his first professional hat-trick in Blues' 3-1 home victory over Rotherham United in October 2018. As of the end of the 2018/19 season, he had managed 32 goals in 125 Birmingham City matches since arriving from Burnley in 2017.

HARLEE
DEAN

Like Maxime, Harlee is another former Brentford player who arrived at St. Andrew's in 2017. The defender featured in 82 matches and scored twice in his first two seasons as a Birmingham City player, having previously netted ten times in 249 appearances for the Bees between 2012 and 2017.

DAVID
STOCKDALE

Since making his senior debut for York City in 2003, David has made over 400 club appearances for the likes of Darlington, Fulham, Rotherham United (loan), Leicester City (loan), Plymouth Argyle (loan), Ipswich Town, Hull City (loan) and Brighton & Hove Albion. Since signing for Birmingham City in 2017, he was loaned to Southend United, Wycombe Wanderers and Coventry City.

JAKE
CLARKE-SALTER

Chelsea starlet Jake will spend the 2019/20 season on loan with Birmingham City. The Carshalton-born defender was a member of the England squad that won the 2017 FIFA Under-20 World Cup while he captained the Young Lions at the 2019 UEFA European Under-21 Championships. Since making his senior debut for Chelsea against Aston Villa in 2016, Jake has been loaned to Bristol Rovers, Sunderland and Dutch side SBV Vitesse.

FRAN
VILLALBA

Fran is another of Birmingham City's Spanish contingent, with the forward having joined Blues from Valencia in the summer of 2019. The highly regarded midfielder has represented Spain at all levels between Under-16 and Under-19 and made his senior debut for Valencia B at the age of just 16. Fran signed for Blues on a free transfer, putting pen-to-paper on a three-year contract with the club.

KERIM
MRABTI

Kerim arrived at Birmingham City in the January 2019 transfer window and signed an 18-month contract with the club. He made his Blues debut in a 2-0 win over Nottingham Forest in February 2019 and got his first goal for the club in a 3-1 win at Rotherham United a few months later. The versatile player had won three senior caps for Sweden by the end of the 2018/19 season.

JACQUES
MAGHOMA

Jacques has featured in over 150 matches for Birmingham City since joining the club from Sheffield Wednesday in 2015. The DR Congo international is a former Tottenham Hotspur trainee who made a name for himself at Burton Albion, where he was included in the PFA League Two Team of the Year in 2012/13.

GARY
GARDNER

Craig's brother Gary spent a successful loan spell with Birmingham City during the 2018/19 season, scoring two goals in 42 matches. The midfielder made his move from city rivals Aston Villa to St. Andrew's permanent in the summer of 2019. The Solihull-born player is a former England Under-21 international.

AGUS
MEDINA

Agus – or Agustin Medina Delgado to give his full name – is a former product of Valencia CF's youth system. The versatile player, who can operate at both right-back and in midfielder, turned out for the likes of Sabadell B, Sabadell, Celta B and Cornella at the start of his career prior to signing for Blues in the summer of 2019. The Spaniard made his Birmingham City debut against Portsmouth in the 2019/20 Carabao Cup.

MOHA
RAMOS

Moha agreed to join Blues on a season-long loan from Real Madrid in the summer of 2019. The young goalkeeper, who first appeared in Los Blancos at the age of 17, was brought in to provide competition to the likes of Lee Camp, David Stockdale and Connal Trueman for the Birmingham City number one shirt.

ALVARO
GIMENEZ

Spanish forward Alvaro joined Birmingham City in the summer of 2019, having bagged an impressive 20 goals in 39 league matches for UD Almeria which made him the Segunda Division's top goal scorer in 2018/19. The former Spain Under-17 international has previously represented the likes of Elche, Valencia B, Torrellano Illice, Mallorca and Alcorcon during a well-travelled career.

DAVID
DAVIS

An ankle injury sustained in July 2018 saw David miss a large part of the 2018/19 season. He returned to action as a substitute for Blues' home match with Bolton Wanderers in February 2019 and subsequently featured in ten further games before the end of the campaign. At the time of writing, he was closing in on his 200th appearance for the club having signed from Wolverhampton Wanderers back in 2014.

CONNAL
TRUEMAN

A product of Blues' Academy, Connal featured in two EFL Championship matches during the 2018/19 season, making his senior debut for the club against Norwich City in August 2018. The Birmingham-born stopper has previously spent loan spells with non-league sides Leamington and Solihull Moors.

CHARLIE
LAKIN

Box-to-box midfielder Charlie is one of Birmingham City's brightest young prospects. The player made his senior debut in an FA Cup tie against Huddersfield Town in February 2018 and subsequently featured in ten EFL Championship matches in 2018/19.

IVAN
SUNJIC

Croatian international Ivan signed a five-year contract with Birmingham City in July 2019 having arrived from Dinamo Zagreb. The midfielder captained Croatia at the 2019 UEFA European Under-21 Championships in Italy having also made his debut for his country against Mexico in May that year. Born in Zenica, Bosnia and Herzegovina, Ivan spent two spells with Zagreb-based side NK Lokomotiva earlier in his career.

STEVE
SEDDON

Steve was loaned to Stevenage and AFC Wimbledon during the 2018/19 season as he looked to build experience and stake a claim for inclusion in Blues' first-team. The defender scored three goals in 25 appearances for Stevenage and netted three more times in 18 matches for the Dons during the campaign.

JEFFERSON
MONTERO

Jefferson started his career with Emelec and Independiente Valle in his native Ecuador before signing for La Liga outfit Villarreal in 2009. After loan spells with fellow Spanish sides Levante and Real Betis, the winger joined Mexican outfit Morelia in 2012 prior to joining his current parent club Swansea City in 2014. The player, who featured for Ecuador at the 2014 FIFA World Cup, is on loan at Birmingham City until the end of the 2019/20 season.

BIRMINGHAM CITY
TEAM PHOTO 2019/20

WORDSEARCH

CAN YOU FIND THE SURNAMES OF EIGHT CURRENT
& FORMER BLUES STRIKERS...

ADAMS	FRANCIS	LATCHFORD
ADEBOLA	HESKEY	LEEK
CLARIDGE	JUTKIEWICZ	

```
Z  C  I  W  E  I  K  T  U  J
F  D  F  N  M  B  B  Q  H  B
D  R  O  F  H  C  T  A  L  N
C  L  A  R  I  D  G  E  N  A
N  H  S  N  H  T  Y  Q  L  R
G  E  M  Y  C  M  X  O  J  C
M  S  A  L  R  I  B  Q  L  K
P  K  D  K  F  E  S  E  X  N
V  E  A  Q  D  X  E  D  G  W
M  Y  X  A  M  K  Q  H  Q  M
```

ANSWERS ON PAGE 60

SUMMER SIGNINGS
2019

BIRMINGHAM CITY WERE ONE OF THE BUSIEST EFL CHAMPIONSHIP CLUBS IN THE 2019 SUMMER TRANSFER WINDOW, BRINGING A HOST OF NEW PLAYERS TO ST. ANDREW'S TRILLION TROPHY STADIUM.

Following a successful loan spell with Blues during the 2018/19 season, **Gary Gardner** made his move from Aston Villa a permanent one, putting pen-to-paper on a three-year contract at St. Andrews.

No less than four Spanish players arrived at St. Andrew's during the summer. Winger **Ivan Guzman** joined on a free transfer, having spent the previous two seasons with Catalan side UE Olot. The Badalona-born player was loaned to Blues' sister club UE Cornella for the 2019/20 season. Compatriot **Agus Medina** arrived from Cornella, making his Birmingham City debut at Portsmouth in the Carabao Cup in August 2019.

Fellow Spaniard **Alvaro Gimenez** signed for Blues having been the top scorer in the Spanish Segunda Division in 2018/19 with 20 goals in 39 league matches for UD Almeria. Midfielder **Fran Villalba**, who has represented Spain at various youth and development levels, agreed a three-year contract with Birmingham City after leaving his home city club, Valencia CF.

Former Arsenal trainee **Dan Crowley** made his Birmingham City debut in the 1-0 win at Brentford on the opening day of the 2019/20 EFL Championship season having joined from Dutch side Willem II. Crowley was substituted in the second-half of that match and replaced by fellow new arrival **Ivan Sunjic**. The Croatian international – who captained his country at the 2019 UEFA European Under-21 Championships – signed for Blues from Dinamo Zagreb.

Birmingham City also entered the loan market to bring **Jake Clarke-Salter**, **Moha Ramos** and **Jefferson Montero** to St. Andrew's for the 2019/20 season. Chelsea defender Clarke-Salter was a FIFA Under-20 World Cup winner with England in 2017 and captained the Young Lions at the UEFA European Under-21 Championships two years later. Real Madrid's Ramos presented manager Pep Clotet with a wealth of goalkeeping options with Lee Camp, David Stockdale and Connal Trueman all on the books at St. Andrew's.

Ecuador international Montero joined Blues on loan from Swansea City, who he previously represented in the Premier League. The winger has spent loan spells with Spanish club Getafe, Ecuadorian side Emelec and fellow EFL Championship side West Bromwich Albion in recent years.

Amongst those to depart the club during the summer transfer window were **Jota**, **Che Adams**, **Michael Morrison**, **Cheikh Ndoye**, **Viv Solomon-Otabar** and **Issac Vassell** while **Jake Weaver** and **Josh Dacres-Cogley** went on loan.

#FABRICOFTHECITY

INTRODUCING BIRMINGHAM CITY'S 2019/20 HOME KIT.

Birmingham City unveiled their home strip for the 2019/20 season at the National Trust-owned Birmingham Back to Backs. The kit launch, which ran with the social media hashtag #FabricOfTheCity, took inspiration from the hit television series 'Peaky Blinders'. Blues players dressed in flat caps for the occasion and wore suits from Garrison Tailors – the same suppliers used by the BBC show.

Produced by adidas, the home shirt is designed with the club's famous royal blue and accompanied with a striking yellow trim. A darker, navy shade can be found on the sleeves while adidas' trademark three stripes can be found across the shoulders. The white shorts feature blue stripes while the socks are blue with white detail.

LUCAS **JUTKIEWICZ**

GETTING **SHIRTY**

A LOOK AT SOME MEMORABLE BIRMINGHAM CITY KIT DESIGNS OVER THE YEARS…

Kit History

Formed in 1875 as Small Heath Alliance, Birmingham City played in a blue shirt with a white diagonal sash and white shorts in their early history. They also sported some unusual home shirts towards the latter part of the 19th century, including a gold and black striped shirt used for the opening matches of the 1890/91 season and a sky-blue top worn between 1893 and 1900.

From 1901 through to 1965, the club's kit consisted of the traditional blue shirts and white shorts – although some shirts had a white 'V' on them while some had collars and some didn't. For the second part of 1960s, Birmingham City wore blue shorts before reintroducing white shorts along with a radically different shirt design in 1971…

1971-1975

Kit:
HOME
Manufacturer:
UMBRO
Sponsor:
NONE

In 1971, Birmingham City launched one of their most iconic kits of all-time, which incorporated the so-called 'penguin' shirt. Manufactured by Umbro, the blue shirt featured a broad white vertical panel down the front and was usually worn with white shorts. The kit remains a popular one with Blues fans as it was worn when the club got promoted to the old First Division in 1972 and was worn by legendary players such as Bob Latchford and Trevor Francis. The 'penguin' style shirt has been revisited by Blues over the decades, with the home kits of 1997/98, 2007/08 and 2009/10 paying homage to a real club classic.

1972-1974

Kit:
THIRD
Manufacturer:
UMBRO
Sponsor:
NONE

One of Birmingham City's most famous outfits over the years has to be its first-ever third kit, which included a shirt featuring the colours of the German national flag – black, red and yellow. It is believed this kit was introduced for Blues' tour of West Germany in 1972 and was subsequently worn by the players in a number of away games over a two-year period, including First Division matches at Queens Park Rangers, Tottenham Hotspur and West Bromwich Albion.

GETTING **SHIRTY**

1977-1980

Kit:
AWAY
Manufacturer:
ADIDAS
Sponsor:
NONE

In 1977, Birmingham City began working with current kit manufacturers adidas for the first time. Both home and away kits launched for the 1977/78 season featured round neck collars and the German company's famous three stripes on both the shirt and shorts. With Blues having worn an all-yellow kit for the first time in 1976/77 under previous manufacturers Umbro, adidas continued with the colour theme in 1977 and designed one of the club's most popular away kits to date.

1992-1993

Kit:
HOME
Manufacturer:
INFLUENCE
Sponsor:
TRITON SHOWERS

It's fair to say Birmingham City had a number of loud kits during the 1990s - the home and away numbers worn during the 1991/92 season being a case in point. Nothing could top the sheer exuberance of the 1992/93 home kit by Influence though. An all-blue kit featuring splashes of yellow, green and navy meant there was no missing Blues players on the pitch that campaign, even if the floodlights failed! In true Marmite fashion, some fans loved the kit, others hated it!

1986-1987

Kit:
AWAY
Manufacturer:
MATCHWINNER
Sponsor:
CO-OP MILK

Birmingham City's shirt first featured a sponsor in 1983, following a deal with brewers, Ansells. The next logo to appear on it was 'Co-op Milk' between 1986 and 1988. One of the most unusual Blues kits emerged during this time – an away design featuring a two-tone grey shirt with blue vertical box along with blue shorts featuring a grey trim.

1994-1995

Kit:
AWAY
Manufacturer:
ADMIRAL
Sponsor:
TRITON SHOWERS

Continuing the theme of quirky 1990s football kits is Blues' away attire from the 1994/95 season. Manufactured by Admiral, the red shirt featured an unusual black and white pattern at the bottom. Having won the old Second Division title and the Football League Trophy that campaign, supporters continue to have fond memories of the kit.

GETTING **SHIRTY**

1995-1996

Kit:
HOME
Manufacturer:
ADMIRAL
Sponsor:
AUTO WINDSCREENS

Admiral produced some other stand-out kits for Birmingham City, including the home and away numbers for the 1995/96 season. The red away shirt featured vertical blue and white lines across it while the home shirt had the words 'The Blues' and the club's original crest woven into its material. Complete with a white collar, online football shirt bloggers 'Football Shirt Collective' have dubbed it "the most glorious Birmingham City shirt to be worn at St. Andrew's".

2002-2003

Kit:
HOME
Manufacturer:
LE COQ SPORTIF
Sponsor:
PHONES 4U

Birmingham City sported a simple and stylish home kit for their inaugural season in the Premier League in 2002/03. The shirt featured a 'V' neck collar with the club's traditional royal blue incorporated on both the top and shorts with white socks. Blues enjoyed home and away victories over rivals Aston Villa during the campaign in which they finished 13th in the table.

1997-1998

Kit:
HOME
Manufacturer:
PONY
Sponsor:
AUTO WINDSCREENS

In 1997, Pony became the first manufacturer to bring back Birmingham City's 'penguin'-style home shirt of the 1970s. With Paul Furlong and new signing Dele Adebola knocking in the goals for fun in this kit during the 1997/98 season, Blues were unlucky not to make it into the First Division play-offs that campaign as they finished seventh.

2010-2011

Kit:
HOME
Manufacturer:
XTEP
Sponsor:
F&C INVESTMENTS

This kit will forever hold a special place in the hearts of Birmingham City supporters as it was worn in Blues' 2-1 victory over Arsenal in the League Cup Final on 27 February 2011. Nigerian striker Obafemi Martins came off the bench to score the winner in the match.

GETTING SHIRTY

2011-2012

Kit:
THIRD
Manufacturer:
XTEP
Sponsor:
RATIONALFX

Birmingham City gained some notable results in their 2011/12 third kit, including 2-1 away wins at SC Braga and NK Maribor in the UEFA Europa League. This yellow and white number became Blues' default 'away' kit for the campaign, as their official away strip of dark grey and teal was only ever worn during that pre-season and has since become something of a collectors' item!

2015-2016

Kit:
HOME
Manufacturer:
CARBRINI
Sponsor:
EZE GROUP

As Birmingham City celebrated their 140th anniversary in 2015, manufacturers Carbrini launched a home kit that strongly resembled the strip originally worn by Small Heath Alliance following the club's foundation in 1875. The blue shirt included a white sash which was printed with the names of all supporters who pre-bought a special 'Woven in History' package.

2012-2013

Kit:
THIRD
Manufacturer:
DIADORA
Sponsor:
EZE GROUP

Perhaps inspired by Sicilian club US Citta di Palermo, Italian manufacturers introduced a pink shirt with black shorts and socks as Birmingham City's third kit for the 2012/13 season. The kit was worn in matches including a 3-3 draw at Millwall and a 2-2 tie at Leicester City during the campaign.

2018-2019

Kit:
AWAY
Manufacturer:
ADIDAS
Sponsor:
888 SPORT

adidas paid homage to the classic away kit they produced for Birmingham City back in 1977 with another spectacular design worn on the road in 2018/19. The bright yellow shirt featured a round-neck and a blue trim while the blue shorts incorporated three yellow stripes on each side.

WHO ARE YA?!

GUESS THE IDENTITY OF THESE PAST AND PRESENT BLUES PLAYERS FROM THE FOLLOWING CLUES…

ANSWERS ON PAGE 60

PLAYER 1

I am a goalkeeper and I featured in 44 of Blues' 46 EFL Championship matches in 2018/19. I played for England Under-21s between 2004 and 2007 before going on to represent Northern Ireland at senior international level. My former clubs include Derby County, Queens Park Rangers, Nottingham Forest and AFC Bournemouth.

PLAYER 2

I was born in Plymouth in 1954 and I scored 12 goals in 52 appearances for England between 1977 and 1986. I was Birmingham City's top goal scorer for three season campaigns between 1975 and 1978 became the first English footballer to command a transfer fee of £1m when I left Blues for Nottingham Forest in 1979.

PLAYER 4

I spent the 2018/19 season on loan with Birmingham City before signing for the club permanently in the summer of 2019. I am a midfielder and I scored twice in five appearances for England Under-21s between 2011 and 2012. My brother is also a professional footballer.

PLAYER 3

I am a versatile player and I can play as either a left-back or left-winger. I joined Birmingham City in the summer of 2018 and I made 39 appearances in my debut season with the club. Early in my career, I won five caps for Denmark Under-21s.

WHO ARE YA?!

PLAYER 5

I was born in Huddersfield on 14 August 1986. I scored 42 goals in 202 appearances for Birmingham City between 2006 and 2011. My strike for Blues in a 2-2 draw at Liverpool was voted BBC Match of the Day's 'Goal of the Month' for November 2009.

PLAYER 6

I was born in Zaire and joined Tottenham Hotspur's youth academy when I was just 15 years of age. I joined Blues in 2015 and I have since made over 150 appearances for the club. I am a DR Congo international.

PLAYER 7

I retired from playing in 2018, having represented the likes of Inter Milan, Newcastle United and VfL Wolfsburg during my career. I only played six matches on loan for Birmingham City in 2011, but I scored a famous goal for the club at Wembley Stadium during that time. I netted 19 times in 42 senior international matches for Nigeria between 2004 and 2015.

PLAYER 8

I was born in Aylesbury, Buckinghamshire on 9 May 1989. I am a striker and I scored 23 goals in 26 FA Women's Super League appearances for Birmingham City Women between 2017 and 2019. I have made over 80 appearances for the England national team and I was Blues' top-scorer in 2018/19 before departing the club for Manchester City Women.

47

SUPER STARS

Before the start of the 2018/19 FA WSL season, Birmingham City Women gained a credible point against Manchester City in their opening Continental Cup Group One North match of the campaign. The visitors to the Automated Technology Group (ATG) Stadium in Solihull, where Blues continue to play their home matches, picked up a bonus point with a 5-4 penalty shoot-out victory.

A 2-0 victory over rivals Aston Villa in the second group stage gave Blues maximum points and local bragging rights thanks to second half goals from Kerys Harrop and Charlie Wellings.

It took just 42 seconds to open their 2018/19 FA WSL goal scoring account in a 1-0 home victory over Everton in September 2018. Ellen White played a neat through-ball into the path of Charlie Wellings, who finished from close range. The team's impressive start to the season continued with a 2-0 Continental Cup triumph at Sheffield United and 1-0 wins over Brighton & Hove Albion and Reading in the FA WSL.

"IT TOOK JUST 42 SECONDS TO OPEN THEIR 2018/19 FA WSL GOAL SCORING ACCOUNT."

After a 3-2 home defeat to Manchester City in the league, Blues Women returned to winning ways with a 1-0 triumph at Bristol City, which saw Aoife Mannion score her second FA WSL goal of the campaign. October 2018 ended with a goalless draw with Chelsea.

Birmingham City Women were beaten 3-1 by eventual FA WSL champions Arsenal in November 2018 but bounced back quickly to beat West Ham United 3-0 in their next game with Kerys Harrop, Emma Follis and Lucy Staniforth on target that afternoon. Follis and Connie Scofield scored in a 2-0 away win at Liverpool thereafter in a match played at Tranmere Rovers' Prenton Park stadium.

December 2018 began with a hard-fought 2-1 success over Yeovil Town. Goals from Staniforth and Wellings secured the points, while Emily Syme's stoppage time strike for the Glovers ultimately proved to be nothing more than a consolation.

Blues Women's biggest win of the campaign followed a few days later with a 6-0 hammering of Leicester City in the Continental Cup. The team secured progress to the knockout phase of the competition with a goalless home draw with Bristol City in their final group stage match.

2019 started with a 2-1 home win over Reading as Birmingham City Women continued hot on the tails of FA WSL pacesetters Arsenal and Manchester City at the top of the division. They were eliminated from the Continental Cup with a 2-1 defeat at Arsenal during January though and suffered a 1-0 loss at home to Bristol City in the league.

That defeat proved to be the final match in charge for manager Marc Skinner, who departed to take the top job at one of the biggest club's in the women's game, Orlando Pride. The Florida team's squad at the time of writing includes Brazil's multiple-World Player of the Year Marta Tejedor and United States international Alex Morgan.

Marta Tejedor was announced as Skinner's replacement, meaning six of the 11 FA WSL sides had female bosses at that stage of the season. In her first match in charge on 27 January 2019, Birmingham City Women achieved arguably their best result of the campaign, winning 3-2 at Chelsea. Having gone behind to a strike from Erin Cuthbert, Blues levelled through Emma Follis and took a second-half lead thanks to an effort from Lucy Quinn. Cuthbert equalised for the Londoners late-on before a dramatic winner from Ellen White in the third minute of stoppage time at the end of the game.

After a 3-1 away win at Yeovil Town in the FA Women's Cup fourth round, Birmingham City Ladies bowed out of the competition with a 2-1 defeat at Reading in round five. Defeats to Brighton & Hove Albion and Arsenal followed in the league but Blues Women ended their FA WSL campaign in style with four successive wins. A goal from Hayley Ladd and a brace from White saw them win 3-1 at Everton while strikes from Ladd and Chloe Arthur helped Tejedor's side to a 2-1 win at West Ham United.

"TEJEDOR WAS PRESENTED WITH THE DIVISION'S FINAL MANAGER OF THE MONTH."

2-0 wins at home to Liverpool and away to Yeovil Town confirmed Birmingham City Women's fourth-place finish in the FA WSL in 2018/19. Tejedor was presented with the division's final Manager of the Month award of the campaign for April 2019.

At the end of the season, Birmingham City Ladies confirmed a two-year extension to their contract to play home matches at Solihull Moors' Automated Technology Group (ATG) Stadium – now known as the SportsNation.bet Stadium. A redevelopment programme took place at the ground during the summer months, with a new main stand, players' tunnel and home and away dugouts constructed. It was also confirmed that Blues Women will train at St. Andrew's Trillion Trophy Training Centre at Wast Hills and share the same facilities as the men's team at Wast Hills on a permanent basis.

Full details on Birmingham City Women, including fixture and ticketing information, can be found at...
www.bcfc.com/womens-team

49

BLUES WOMEN
STAR PLAYERS

HANNAH **HAMPTON**

POSITION: Goalkeeper
JOINED BLUES: 2016
PREVIOUS CLUB(S):
N/A

Hannah represents her home city club, having been born in Birmingham on 16 November 2000. The young goalkeeper started her career as a forward at the **Villarreal CF** academy in Spain - which she attended from the age of five - before switching position. Hannah moved back to England in 2010 to join **Stoke City** before her transfer to Blues in 2016. The **England** Under-19 stopper made her **Birmingham City** debut against **Doncaster Belles** on 5 November 2017.

KERYS **HARROP**

POSITION: Defender
JOINED BLUES: 2011
PREVIOUS CLUB(S):
None

Blues' longest-serving Women's player and captain, Kerys progressed through the club's Centre of Excellence before making her FA WSL debut in 2011. **Birmingham City** were League and Continental Cup runners-up in her first two seasons at the club, while she got her hands on her first winners' medal in 2012 in the FA Women's Cup. Kerys has a first-class Honours degree from Loughborough University in Sport Science and a Masters Degree and PGCE Teaching Degree from the University of Wolverhampton.

CONNIE **SCOFIELD**

POSITION: Midfielder
JOINED BLUES: 2016
PREVIOUS CLUB(S):
N/A

Born in London on 26 May 1000, Connie joined Blues Women's development centre at the age of nine. The midfielder rose through the ranks to make her senior debut in 2016, putting pen-to-paper on her first professional contract with the club two years later. She has represented **England** at Under-17 and Under-19 level.

CHLOE **ARTHUR**

POSITION: Midfielder
JOINED BLUES: 2018
PREVIOUS CLUB(S):
Celtic, Hibernian, Bristol City

Chloe was included in **Scotland**'s squad for the 2019 FIFA Women's World Cup and featured in their clash with **England** in the opening Group D match at the tournament. The former **Celtic** and **Hibernian** midfielder signed for Blues from FA WSL rivals **Bristol City** ahead of the start of the 2018/19 season and featured in 19 matches in her debut campaign with the club.

LUCY **STANIFORTH**

POSITION: Midfielder
JOINED BLUES: 2018
PREVIOUS CLUB(S):
Sunderland, Notts
County, Bristol
Academy, Liverpool

Former **Sunderland** captain Lucy joined Blues in July 2018 and was a consistent performer in **Birmingham City**'s midfield in her debut season with the club. Her form was rewarded with a place in Phil Neville's **England** squad for the 2019 FIFA Women's World Cup. She came on as a substitute in the 3-0 win over **Cameroon** in the round of 16 on route to the Lionesses reaching the semi-final of the tournament. Football is very much in the blood for Lucy, with her father Gordon having played for **York City** and **Hull City** whilst her brother turned out for **Sheffield Wednesday**.

SARAH **MAYLING**

POSITION: Midfielder
JOINED BLUES: 2017
PREVIOUS CLUB(S):
Aston Villa

Born in Sutton Coldfield on 20 March 1997, Sarah started her career at rivals **Aston Villa** before signing for Blues in 2017. The midfielder has featured for **England** at various youth and development levels, including Under-17, Under-19 and Under-23 while she has made over 50 appearances for **Birmingham City** in all competitions to date. She played in every match for Blues on route to the FA Women's Cup Final in 2017, including the final itself against **Manchester City**.

RACHEL **WILLIAMS**

POSITION: Forward
JOINED BLUES: 2017
PREVIOUS CLUB(S):
Leicester City,
Doncaster Rovers,
Chelsea, Notts County

Rachel is currently in her second spell with **Birmingham City**, having previously scored 21 goals in 38 league appearances for Blues between 2011 and 2013. The forward was one of the first 17 female players to be given central contracts by The Football Association in May 2009, a few months before she made her debut for **England** against **Iceland** at the Colchester Community Stadium. In addition to playing for Lionesses during her career, Rachel was included in **Great Britain**'s 18-player squad for the 2012 Olympic Games.

CLAUDIA **WALKER**

POSITION: Forward
JOINED BLUES: 2019
PREVIOUS CLUB(S):
Liverpool, Everton

Claudia spent the part of the 2018/19 season on loan with **Birmingham City**, netting once in 17 appearances. The former **England** Under-17 and Under-19 player - who has also featured for the Lionesses' Under-23s - made her move from **Everton** a permanent one in the summer of 2019. She was part of **Liverpool**'s squad that won the FA WSL in 2014, pipping Blues to the title on a dramatic last day.

BLUES WOMEN FA WSL HOME MATCHES 2020

(Home matches at Solihull Moors' SportsNation.bet Stadium)

JAN 19: MANCHESTER CITY. **FEB 9:** BRIGHTON & HOVE ALBION. **FEB 23:** BRISTOL CITY.
APR 5: WEST HAM UNITED. **APR 26:** ARSENAL.

Fixture dates are subject to change – visit **www.bcfc.com/womens-team** for up to date information.

ST. ANDREW'S
TRILLION TROPHY STADIUM

HISTORY

St. Andrew's has been home to Birmingham City Football Club for over a century. The first-ever match at the venue was staged on Boxing Day 1906, when Blues played out a goalless draw with Middlesbrough in front of a crowd of 32,000.

The ground has hosted nine FA Cup semi-finals to date – the first producing a 3-1 win for The Wednesday over Woolwich Arsenal in 1907 while the most recent saw Leicester City triumph 2-0 against Sheffield United in 1961.

After Birmingham City purchased the freehold of St. Andrew's in 1921, a series of major developments followed including the erection of roofs over the Kop and Railway End Terraces. The stadium welcomed its record attendance of 66,844 (some sources list it as 67,341) for Blues' FA Cup fifth round tie against Everton on 11 February 1939. The existing Main Stand at St. Andrew's opened in 1952, while floodlights were installed at the ground for the first time in 1956.

The present day Kop and Tilton

Road stands were opened in the mid-1990s, while the newest stand, the two-tier Gil Merrick Stand was completed in 2009. The seating capacity of the ground - which has been known as St. Andrew's Trillion Trophy Stadium since the summer of 2018 - is 29,409.

"THE GROUND HAS HOSTED NINE FA CUP SEMI-FINALS TO DATE"

MATCH DAY

FULL INFORMATION ON PURCHASING TICKETS FOR BIRMINGHAM CITY HOME MATCHES CAN BE FOUND AT
WWW.BCFC.COM/TICKETS/TICKET
THE WEBSITE ALSO HAS DETAILS ON STADIUM TOURS.

The nearest railway station to the stadium is Bordesley on the North Warwickshire Line (Birmingham Moor Street to Stratford-upon-Avon), which is served by regular services on matchday. The stadium is approximately a 30-minute walk from Birmingham New Street station and 20-minutes from Birmingham Coach Station.

THE CLUB'S ADDRESS IS;
ST. ANDREW'S TRILLION TROPHY STADIUM, BIRMINGHAM, B9 4RL

Further matchday information can be found at
www.bcfc.com/tickets/essential-information/getting-to-the-ground

BLUES
SUPER QUIZ

1 IN WHAT YEAR WERE BIRMINGHAM CITY FOOTBALL CLUB FOUNDED AS 'SMALL HEATH ALLIANCE'?

2 How many times have Birmingham City won the Football League Cup during their history and in what years?

3 WHAT NATIONALITY IS BLUES DEFENDER MAXIME COLIN?

4 Between New Year's Day and 9 February 2019, how many consecutive EFL Championship matches did Che Adams score for Birmingham City?

5 WHICH SPORTSWEAR FIRM MANUFACTURES BIRMINGHAM CITY'S KITS?

6 WHO SCORED A HAT-TRICK FOR BLUES IN THEIR 3-1 VICTORY OVER ROTHERHAM UNITED ON 6 OCTOBER 2018?

7 Who did Birmingham City beat 4-2 on penalties in the First Division Play-Off Final of 12 May 2002?

8 IN WHICH YEARS (TWO) WERE BIRMINGHAM CITY FA CUP RUNNERS-UP?

9 WHO SCORED BLUES' WINNING GOAL IN THE 1995 FOOTBALL LEAGUE TROPHY FINAL?

10 Which Premier League club did Blues face in a pre-season friendly at St. Andrew's Trillion Trophy Stadium on 27 July 2019?

11 IN WHICH CAPITAL CITY DID BLUES TAKE ON LIVERPOOL IN THE 2001 FOOTBALL LEAGUE CUP FINAL?

12 What season did Blues win the old Second Division (third-tier of English league football) title?

13 With 267 strikes in 445 appearances for Birmingham City between 1920 and 1935, who is the club's top, all-time goal scorer?

14 WHO WROTE BIRMINGHAM CITY'S FAMOUS ANTHEM, 'KEEP RIGHT ON TO THE END OF THE ROAD'?

15 FROM WHICH CLUB DID BIRMINGHAM CITY SIGN MICHAEL MORRISON?

ANSWERS ON PAGE 60

DAVID **DAVIS**

PRE-SEASON 2019
TRAINING CAMP

2019/20
PRE-SEASON
ROUND-UP

CD COVA DA PIEDADE 1
BLUES 1

Blues started their pre-season preparations by competing in two matches in the Torneio Internacional do Sado in Setubal, Portugal. Marc Roberts gave Pep Clotet's side a deserved half-time lead against CD Cova da Piedade but with less than a minute of normal time remaining, Guinea-Bissau international Leocisio Sami got the equaliser for the Portuguese second division outfit. Cova won 4-3 in the ensuing penalty shootout.

VITORIA SETUBAL 2
BLUES 2

Birmingham City's second and final match in the Torneio Internacional do Sado was an entertaining 2-2 draw with Portuguese top-flight team Vitoria Setubal at the Estadio do Bonfim. Lukas Jutkiewicz gave Blues an early lead in the match with a close-range header before Zequinha's 23rd-minute leveller for Vitoria. Kristian Pedersen put Clotet's side 2-1 up in the second-half, but Blues were again pegged back as Khalid Hachadi equalised. Setubal triumphed 5-3 on penalties to lift the trophy, having won their second successive shootout at the tournament.

BLUES 6
SWINDON TOWN 1

Blues romped to an impressive 6-1 victory over League Two side Swindon Town in a behind-closed-doors match at the Trillion Trophy Training Centre. Dan Crowley scored the opener on his first Birmingham City appearance while Isaac Vassell, Odin Bailey and Craig Gardner also got on the scoresheet to put Pep Clotet's team 4-0 up by half-time. Michael Doughty pulled a goal back for the Robins in the second-half before a brace from Jude Bellingham completed Blues' convincing win.

BRISTOL ROVERS 1
BLUES 2

Having fallen behind to a fifth-minute strike from Kyle Bennett, Birmingham City recovered to keep up their unbeaten run in pre-season. Blues levelled seven minutes later through a close-range effort from Kristian Pedersen, who scored from the rebound after a save from Anssi Jaakkola. Lukas Jutkiewicz got the winner early in the second period with a powerful header.

BLUES 0
BRIGHTON & HOVE ALBION 4

Blues were well beaten in their final pre-season fixture by Premier League side Brighton & Hove Albion. Goals from Glenn Murray and Jurgen Locadia and a brace from Shane Duffy gave the Seagulls a convincing win in front of a crowd of 4,846 at St. Andrew's Trillion Trophy Stadium.

ANSWERS

P38. WORDSEARCH

```
Z  C  I  W  E  I  K  T  U  J
F  D  F  N  M  B  B  Q  H  B
D  R  O  F  H  C  T  A  L  N
C  L  A  R  I  D  G  E  N  A
N  H  S  N  H  T  Y  Q  L  R
G  E  M  Y  C  M  X  O  J  C
M  S  A  L  R  I  B  Q  L  K
P  K  D  K  F  E  S  E  X  N
V  E  A  Q  D  X  E  D  G  W
M  Y  X  A  M  K  Q  H  Q  M
```

P46-47. WHO ARE YA?!

Player 1 – Lee Camp
Player 2 – Trevor Francis
Player 3 – Kristian Pedersen
Player 4 – Gary Gardner

Player 5 – Cameron Jerome
Player 6 – Jacques Maghoma
Player 7 – Obafemi Martins
Player 8 – Ellen White

P54. BLUES SUPER QUIZ

1) 1875
2) Twice – in 1963 and 2011
3) French
4) Six
5) adidas

6) Lukas Jutkiewicz
7) Norwich City
8) 1931 and 1956
9) Paul Tait
10) Brighton & Hove Albion

11) Cardiff
12) 1994/95
13) Joe Bradford
14) Sir Henry 'Harry' Lauder
15) Charlton Athletic

IVAN**SUNJIC**

WHERE'S BEAU BRUMMIE?